The Way i Look at You

LAVANYA AGARWAL

BLUEROSE PUBLISHERS
India | U.K.

For permissions requests or inquiries regarding this publication, please contact:

BLUEROSE PUBLISHERS
www.BlueRoseONE.com
info@bluerosepublishers.com
+91 8882 898 898
+4407342408967

ISBN: 978-93-7139-674-5

First Edition: May 2025

To all the quite people
with stories in their heads...

Dear Reader,

Just like you I am a hopeless romantic. This world doesn't understand us and they never will. But don't lose hope and don't keep looking for the one. Life has it's own way of revealing itself and maybe you should trust the process just like I do.

I wrote my very first poem in high school and didn't really know that I would eventually fall in love with writing at that time. It was a sweet escape for me, I believed I could talk through poems. I have met some amazing people through this journey of life who taught me so much. After any minor inconvenience in life, I found myself penning down my thoughts. I have learnt, evolved and moved on leaving every piece of the person I've met in my poems. These writings are my own self-reflection, my own way of understanding things.

I urge the reader to feel every word and understand the true meaning as you turn each page which contains a story behind it. These are emotions from my private life which I am now sharing with you all with the hope that you connect and relate to it. This is the first of many more to come.

Thank you to all the readers for buying a piece of my heart.

Until it was gone

She never realised his love until
Everything was gone
And she sat on the hill
Singing a beautiful song

When she lifted her eyes
There was nothing but fire filled inside

Her strong heart
Had become fragile
And frozen with ice

There was no room for love
Or anything of that kind

Whenever she stopped herself from loving
him
He repeatedly visited her mind

She was losing herself again
Still sitting on the hill alone
Until it started to rain

She allowed herself to think about everything
that took place
She termed it as a "memory"
That she had locked inside a cage

The cage was becoming old and rusty
So she opened it
And tried to love him all over again

But nothing was left except
Her poetry
So full of love and pain

A dandelion

You're a dandelion among the leaves,
Standing alone in the breeze.
You know you're strong,
Even if they considered you wrong.
Promise yourself the spring you deserve,
Because before them,
It's yourself you should serve.

I AM FULL OF LOVE

Our favourite song

I play our favourite song
At 2 am on the street
No one tells me
If I'm doing right or wrong
Or whether insanity has hit me

You are the stars in the night
Or the light on the road outside
You are my favourite cryon
Better than red, blue or neon
You are my diary entries
That I write day long

Hiding you in my words
Is the hardest of all
As it brings out the truth after all

The flower

The flower was left unwatered yesterday
You didn't care
You didn't stay

The flower is slowly withering away
It doesn't need fertile soil, water or sunlight
It needs you, standing by it's side

It's you who let it wither away
After days, you come back
You show all the love, the care
But isn't it too late?

Don't you know that you were the one who got it in the first place
With the brightest of smile on your face
And promised to water it everyday
Where are you now?
Did the love fade away?

Its funny how you water it now
When the stem has got crooked, the petals are falling off, the colour has become pale, the love is gone

Still the flower tries
It tries to bloom
Just for you

YOU MEAN THE WORLD TO ME

Look for yourself

Look for the one when you're in a crowd
Look for peace when the world gets too loud
Look for a house when the world has drowned
Look for a rainbow among all the clouds
Look for yourself
And feel proud

December

I still remember the look on your face
You said it was over
I ran towards the bottom of the hill
My heart turned colder

A fraction of seconds
Had turned me into a devil
I had so many questions
But I ran as fast as I could
To avoid everybody's presence

It seemed like an endless road
With my footprints left behind in the snow
I couldn't feel my legs
They had become fully wet

After running half a mile
I looked up and saw a beautiful rainbow
Which brought a smile
On my face for a while

I stood there alone and thought to myself
This is what happens in life
There is no point in dwelling
About the past that's gone

At that moment I saw a beautiful sparrow

That had been shivering from the cold
The temperature was below zero
It looked beautiful covered with snow

The sky was bright blue
I sat under a spruce tree
And thought about the times when I was young
When I did not care about being hated or loved
It was a whole different world
With no truth to be unfurled

Well times had changed
I no longer felt the same
I held onto my memories
And decided to walk ahead
I no longer believed in fairies
My favourite colour was no longer red

After walking for the next two miles
I started to feel eighteen again
I knew how hard it was to say goodbye
I knew how to detect lies

I followed the lights along the path
It seemed like paradise
That moment I pictured my life in a flash
And remembered the pictures that I had burnt of him
But the ashes were still alive

Reflection

I look into your eyes,
And search for something,
Which reflected once in yours and mine,
But all I see are lies,
While I still search for it in your smile,
Trying to hide the same reflection,
Which was so full of love and light.

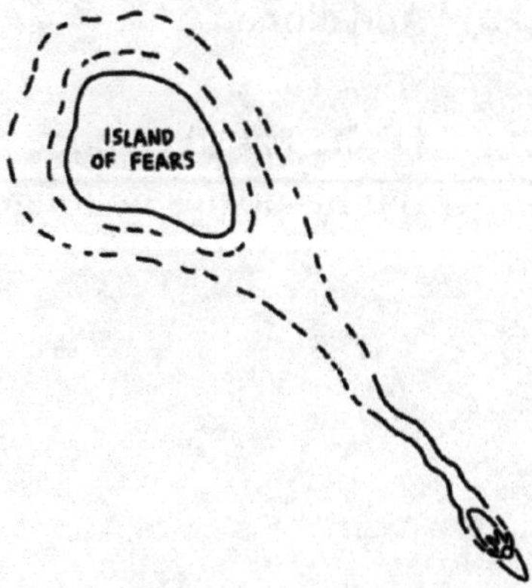
ISLAND
OF FEARS

Muse

He was a poet
And she was his rhyme

She asked him if he could stay a bit longer
But he had no time
He felt bad but left her on the spot
It wasn't his fault
He was scared of getting caught

But the girl failed to realise
And broke out crying
Things started to change
The boy was in a lot of pain

He wrote poems after poems
But couldn't find any words
His love was gone
Everything seemed miserable
And alone

Oh he was still a poet
But his poems no longer rhymed

it's true
what they
say
A place
is only
as good
as the
people in
it

The old me

Whenever I see myself through your eyes
I see the old me
The one I thought no longer existed
But I see it while you drive
Your eyes remain on the road
But my eyes remain locked towards you
I wonder the last time I actually felt alive

It's like a shield
I hardly feel the negativity that surrounds me
sometimes
I let everything go
Something in me says that it's alright
When you're sitting by my side

I do not love you though
It's more than that
It consumes me
It makes me feel like I can do everything I've
always wanted to

You're one of a kind

Lovely things
come and
go
but at least
they come

Destiny, IS IT?

I met him today
He did not get me roses
Like every other guy
Instead he gave me lilies

He took me on a drive
My world seemed so alive
He is the kind of a person who would travel with you for miles
But only when he knows that you're willing to be by his side

He was just like I had imagined him to be
Sweet, caring and sleepy sometimes

They say be with someone who makes everything seem easy
Just by the way they are
And by the way they make you feel

I want to meet him again
And tell him about everything that goes on in my mind

It's all destiny he says
So all I can do is wait

slow down
You really
really really
don't want
to miss
this.

Twisted Love

He is absolutely an old school
The one who would be happy to see you
rule
In the kingdom where everyone seems
cruel
He will be there to support you

He told me he likes white roses
I am ready to steal all of them and give it
to him

But I'm scared to act up too soon
We just started talking
What if he leaves me and goes?

I've decided I'll wait for him
Love is a strange thing
It reaches till the brim
At the first instant
And goes down the next second

But we try, don't we?
Every lock has a different key

He seems the kind of a person who would
kiss you goodnight
And walk out of the room
Closing the lights

He believes that everyone deserves to be happy
And gladly accepts the reality

Does he know that in this artificial world

He reminds me of twisted love?
Where Alex hurts Ava
But they end up together

He doesn't know anything
And he doesn't need to
(For now)

How Love Has Been

Maybe he was right all along
And I was wrong

It isn't you and me against the world
It's just me
And so many things that are left undiscovered

Maybe people do change all of a sudden
We learn that in life we need to run
Not walk for the opportunity to come

Maybe it's time I become a realist
And have a full blown conflict
With my brain who seems to be scared
To take a risk?

Maybe it's time that I come out of the nutshell
That I had created around me

Maybe it's time that I tell you that I'm scared
to let you in
I know how love has been

The battle between my heart and mind is
about to begin
If I let you in
My heart will win
(And I hope it does)

POSITIVE ONLY
BATTERIES DO
NOT WORK

Waiting

I was waiting for the moon to come up at night
It was so dark
I sat on the terrace with a guitar in my hand

The sky looked like a painted canvas
Which was beautiful and blue
It was covered with stars
But all I couldn't see was you

I told the stars everything that I wanted to tell you
So that you would have no clue

As I was waiting
The moon started to show up
He suddenly had to interrupt
And wanted to know if everything I said was true

The moon had been eavesdropping
The stars told the moon that I was upset
Because I missed you

I guess they didn't know that I like being on my own
But if you were here
I would definitely not come here at night everyday
With a guitar in my hand
But be close to you
Somewhere near!

I REMEMBER
EVERYTHING

Boys can be beautiful too

Boys can be beautiful too
In the way they hide bitter truths
And refuse to give up
When life isn't smooth

Boys can be beautiful too
When they surprise someone out of the blue
And refuse to leave if it's too soon

Boys can be beautiful too
With messy hair and a loose t-shirt
Spending time alone on the roof

Boys can be beautiful too
When they cry their eyes out
Because of some bruise

Boys can be beautiful too
In the way they express everything and at the same time they do not
Because they think from their heart
Yes, it's their art

Homecoming

Tear in my eye and a soft smile
As I head out of the airport

I see my car waiting outside
I immediately want to go home

It was freezing cold
But I opened the window to feel the breeze against my skin
I wondered if I feel different
Or is it the same?

I calculate how long it's been
Three months and five days of separation
And tears are already streaming down my face

No matter how much I hide
I know I cannot lie
To myself
When I say I don't miss home

I wonder how everybody's reaction would be
This immediately puts a smile on my face

I reach home and I immediately love myself
Every tear drop is worth falling
As I see my mom
Walking down the stairs

And the days pass
Now when it's time to go back to college
I know it's gonna be hard
But I have to go so that with time I learn and grow

Life is boring without difficulties
Know?

CO2

Waiting for someone
Is like breaking your own heart

I don't know the outcome
Neither do you

But I just know
That if you don't text me again
I will still wish the best for you

Even if you remove me from the little
memories we made
I will still think of you

I tried, u know
I tried to let you go
But couldn't

So if u ever come across this poem
Just know that I miss you

I know you might be thinking I'm crazy
Because we haven't really met each other yet

But if we do, just know
That I really like you

WALK TOGETHER

Better lost

I was so scared to give it away
But I gave you the key
I guess god was testing me again
He wanted to see if I was the same old person or was I changed?

It was the key to my heart
And you lost it in seconds

I don't think I have the right to complain
When I was the one who gave it away

Now the key lies somewhere in the mud
buried
You're not here
I'm looking for it, worried.

Scared that it would come in the wrong hands
Ruining all my future plans

UNLOCK
YOUR
LIMITED
POTENTIAL

YOU

You have your own sparkle,
You have your own circle.
You know the things you hide,
You know the times you've cried,
But it seems that you forgot,
All of it at once,
When others defined you by the things you are not.

•

D o

g o o d

a n d

g o o d

w i l l

c o m e

t o

y o u

•

Beside Your Bed

Will you read me slowly
If I'm the thickest book you find
Or will you rush through
And skip some words between the lines

It is only when you read each chapter twice
that you'll partially unlock the parts that I hide

Will you keep me along with all your books
Or will you keep me separately beside your bed
As years pass by

Will you fall for the facade of my outer covering
Or will you find me in the pages
And truly fall for the words I've written

Everything happens for a reason-
Things go wrong because the universe wants to teach you how to make them right in the future. People you have known for a long time leave because the universe wants you to know that the closest people are sometimes meant to go. People change so that you learn the art to let go. Your environment changes so that you learn to adapt quickly in the next one. You stay with people with different perceptions so that you get to know how important it is to help others and communicate. You go on a walk so that you know how important it is to prioritise yourself. You lose yourself once so that you come back with a greater spirit. You become stronger with every passing day if you believe that everything happens for a reason and that it's important to think positively about everything that's happening around you.

BE HUMAN

TO THE

FULLEST

With love and Hope -

Lavanya Agarwal

whatever happens, I'm letting it
whatever happens, I'm letting it
whatever happens, I'm letting it
whatever happens, I'm letting it
whatever happens, I'm letting it
whatever happens, I'm letting it
whatever happens, I'm letting it
whatever happens, I'm letting it
whatever happens, I'm letting it
whatever happens, I'm letting it
whatever happens, I'm letting it
whatever happens, I'm letting it

to be continued......